WHEN
GOD
SAYS
YES

ISBN: 978-0-578-38731-4

Distributed by Power Of Purpose Publishing

www.PopPublishing.com

Atlanta, Ga. 30326

Content

Dedication

I dedicate this book to God, who is my heavenly Father. Without Him I would not be able to share my story with you.

To my hero, my mom, my best friend, and my pastor thank you for your unconditional love. You have shown me how to really trust in God; and to me that is the greatest gift of all.

To my beautiful, talented, and amazing daughter, because of you I became a better me. You have always been the greatest blessing that God granted me. Like I always say about you, "you have been better to me than ten sons could have ever been."

To my readers and to every woman that has gone through abuse, hold on to the promises of God. Like I always said, "Strong people are made not born." I pray God blesses your lives richly like he has done for me.

The Purpose

My purpose in writing this book is to encourage you to move you forward with love, humility, and compassion for God. I became transparent to give hope to anyone that may be presently where I once was; to give you hope that you can be set free as well. It's not about your greatness but it is all about the greatness of God. This book was also written to empower my readers to know there is nothing you can't do when God Says Yes!

"Whatever God is of; God takes care of." In loving memory of my dear friend who spoke this into my life before the Lord called her home.

I pray this book will bless you as it has blessed me to write it.

Introduction

I said no to the will of God so many times, because of my own fears and doubts. Allowing others judgment about me to be more important than what God the Father says about me. Believe me, His thoughts about me are always better.

"For I know the plans I have for you, declares the LORD, plans to prosper you and not to harm you, plans to give you hope and a future." Jeremiah 29:11

This is what the LORD Almighty, the God of Israel, says to all those He carried into exile from Jerusalem to Babylon. "That he will bring them out and prosper their life."

***The dream*: (I had this dream in 1995).**

One night I had a dream that I was in this condemned building and it was looking as if it was ready for demolition. In this dream, I could see all the faulty wires hanging from the ceiling and the walls. The floors were broken up with large, huge holes in them. The windows were all broken and blown out. The entire building appeared to be an unsafe, dangerous, and hazardous place to be. In this dream, I asked a question, "what am I doing here?" And I heard the voice of the Lord say to me, "this building is you." My face was in dismay and then my eyes closed. When my eyes reopened, I was standing in this beautiful building. It was a beautiful construction and artwork with beautifully structured windows and shining floors and crystal light fixtures. This building was very attractive, pleasant, and inviting. Then I heard the voice of the Lord again saying, "This is you Michelle, when I'm done with you." "First I have to cleanse you from all the sin that you have attached yourself to, then build you up to be the woman of God I created you to be." God made a promise to me that day, that he was going to bring me out of my dilapidated life; restore back to me everything that I lost for getting off track in sin.

"I will repay you for the years the locusts have eaten, the great locust and the young locust, the other locusts and the locust swarm." Joel 2:25

Part 1

God's Plan for Me

In my life, I went through so much and a lot of what I went through was never in the plans of God.

"For I know the plans I have for you, declares the LORD, plans to prosper you and not to harm you, plans to give you hope and a future." Jeremiah 29:11

I heard someone say before, that when someone is going through trials or hardship "that they're just getting their own testimony?" I believe that a lot of it comes from being hard headed and not taking heed to the advice of wisdom that God sends to you through other people in your life. God never planned for us to go through a lot of the heartache and pain that we go through. No, but because of our OWN self-will, we inherit a lot of heartache and pain by the choices that we make.

So often when we come to the Lord, we come in a state where God must get rid of all those bad and unclean habits, those things that are not pleasing unto God, sin that keeps us separated from God; and when we come to Him we must allow Him to create a clean heart in us.

About My Family...

I was born into a family of one handsome brother and three beautiful sisters. Me and my four siblings all have the same mother and father. Yes, my parents were married. Unfortunately, they married too young, which later resulted in separation and ultimately divorce. This was a very difficult time for me as a little girl growing up.

Being raised in a single parent home was one of the hardest things I had to endure in my childhood. Watching my friends living in their homes with both parents always made me feel like something was missing in my life. Watching my mom be the provider, caregiver, the chef, everything in my life. Seeing the strength in my mother as she worked daily to provide for our family was my first lesson in life; she taught me that I can do anything that I set my mind to do, with the help of God. My mom was my first role model of a strong black woman, and there was no one in this entire world I wanted to be like but her.

She taught me that when life throws you a curveball, it's not to destroy you, but to only make you stronger.

However, not having my dad around in my life was a disadvantage for me and often left me feeling like a reject, and mishap. Not feeling wanted, carrying the burden, feeling like my dad was not in my life because of me. The disadvantage of not seeing a complete picture of myself, I saw things in myself that reminded me of my mother's identity, but there was a huge part of me missing that I didn't understand about myself. Not understanding why, I thought and did things the way I did, or why I was the way that I was. Those are some of the things I often thought about as a child. Those were some of the most difficult times in my life.

In the Beginning of My Younger School Years...

Not understanding my parent's separation, it really played a huge role in my behavior when I was a young girl. I stayed in trouble a lot in my early school years. I was carrying the hurt over the absence of my dad, and I took my frustration out in school. I thank God for my teachers and my principal in middle school; they were there for me and saw the good in me. They never gave up hope in me. What I came to learn is that God always sends us what we need. I also thank God for my mother of course being a Christian, she was a praying mother and she never gave up on any of her children, regardless of the trouble we got ourselves into

I was born a Catholic but later my mom converted us to Christianity. At the early age of 12 years old, I accepted Christ as my personal savior into my life, at our home church called; Holy Presence, a part of The Grand old church of God in Christ with one of the greatest pastors of our time. Joining Holy Presence Church gave me stability and grounded me.

I Was So Full of Zeal ...

I was so full of zeal and joy; my youngest sister and I were always telling all our friends about the good news that Jesus Christ Saves. My sister and I would have prayer meetings with our friends at our home, and I tell you we would see the power of God move in our prayer. I loved being in church. Life Was better for me then. Being a Christian, back then we were not allowed to wear pants, makeup, or any worldly apparel. We were taught that we must look and act differently from the world. We were not allowed to listen to secular music, or get involved in anything that was not of God. The bible says, "Wherefore come out from among them, and be ye separate, saith the Lord, and touch not the unclean thing; and I will receive you." Corinthians 6:17. This meant that we were not to look like, or act like the world and not to conform to the things of the world. We must look and act differently, so the world can see the light of God through us.

I remember as a child going to church on Sunday mornings for Sunday school, followed by Sunday morning worship service; go home for dinner and be right back at 7:00 p.m. for Sunday night service Young People Workers Willing (YPWW), back on Tuesday night at 7:00 p.m. Bible Study, Friday night Evangelist service, ending my week on Saturday morning prayer with our First Lady at the church I attended.

I spent most of my young adult life in church and I never complained about going to church. I enjoyed every day of it, it was fun to me; I loved my church and I loved my church family. "Train up a child in the way he should go, and when he is old, he will not depart from it." Proverbs 22:6

I Walked Away from God...

As I got older in my later teens, I walked away from the church and the things of God, thinking that there's so much more to life than going to church all the time. You know when you are around other people who are not being raised like you and don't have the same family values as you do; you see the things that they do, and your mind begins to wonder, what it would be like to experience those things you were not allowed to do in your home. Here is where the seed of curiosity is planted.

Looking back at my life, I have seen so many times how the enemy started his plot against me, just as he does today with our young people. Like I always say, "The devil does not wait till you are too old to fulfill your purpose; No, he starts interfering in your life at a young age, so that he can stop the plan of God from being fulfilled. A good example is when Christ was born. Herod tried to kill Jesus at birth, "Joseph and Mary had been visited by an angel and told that Herod would attempt to kill Jesus, their son. Doing as told, they took their infant son and fled by night into Egypt, where they stayed until Herod had died." Matthew 2:16

It is evident why we have lost so many young people to death and to prison today; to stop the purpose from being fulfilled.

Your self-will can get you in a lot of trouble that you can't get yourself out of, being at the wrong place, at the wrong time, or with the wrong people, can cost you more than you are willing to pay.

The devil sends out his cohort to get you off track by sending out thoughts to you like 'What if "or "I'm grown, I'm going to do what I want to do," or "There's more to life than being a Christian and going to church all the time." Yes, there is, but you need a solid foundation to stand on. "God is the solid rock I stand; all others are sinking sand." This was an old hymn the church used to sing, and is so true. As my grandmother would say "if you don't stand for something, you will fall for anything."

The devil's plan is to stop purpose from being fulfilled because he knows that if your purpose is fulfilled, it will cause many to come to Christ and that's what he doesn't want. He wants as many to join him in hell where his permanent address is and will forever be.

The devil's plans will never work when you are in God. When we belong to God, He will see His plan through regardless of what we go through; God will see you through it all. When we accept Jesus Christ into our heart, we become sons and daughters of God, and the enemy must get permission from the Father to do anything to us;" The Lord said to Satan, "Very well, then, he is in your hands; but you must spare his life." Job 2:6

That gives me the confidence that I will make it out of anything that was plotted against me.

Our Self-Will...

I paid a heavy price because of my own self-will, it almost destroyed me, doing things my way. It took God's Word to restore my mind back to its rightful place. The negative thoughts of myself constantly ran through my mind, reminding me of the absence of my father. Whispering in my ear those thoughts of unworthiness to be loved. That when fake love came, I didn't recognize the difference. The only way you can win the battle in your mind is through the Word of God. "In the beginning was the Word, and the Word was with God, and the Word was God." John 1:1

I began to pick my bible up every day and read what God's Word said about me and for me. You can't just read it, you must believe and agree with what God says about who you are. When I read that I was "fearfully and wonderfully made," Psalm 139:14. My head lifted. When I read that "God doesn't make mistakes. He created me in His image and likeness, and that everything He created was Good! "Genesis 1:27 I realize that I was not a mistake, I was created on purpose, I'm meant to be here.

When I read that "God still has a perfect end for me to prosper me and not to harm me." Jeremiah 29:11. That gave me hope that there was nothing so wrong that I did, that God will not forgive, there was no turning back for me. How fast do you want to live your God-purpose life? That God the Father has proposed and planned just for you?

Part 2

The Detour...

This is where the devil took full advantage of my lack of knowledge and my immaturity of the world. I got into a relationship with a man that was unequally yoked. This was nothing more than a setup and a detour, that took me completely in a different direction from the plan of God; and brought nothing but hurt and pain to my life. I found myself in a place that I never dreamed I would ever be in, nothing but a nightmare from hell.

I was too young to have gone through the things that I went through with this man, for that matter no age should have to endure this. But I thought I was grown. As my grandmother would say, "You're grown enough to make your bed then be grown enough to lie in it." This was not the plan of God for me; no, this was Michelle walking in her own self-will thinking

I knew better. You do know that God gives us our own self will?

I will never forget the first time I took this man to meet my mother when we first started dating. He had brought my mom flowers when he came over the house to meet her. I remember her words till this day when she first laid eyes on him, while she slammed the flowers on the kitchen table. She said, "Michelle this is not the man for you, he will bring you nothing but hurt and pain. You have not been where this man has been, you know nothing about that life. If you continue in this relationship with him, he will bring you down." she went on to say that "she recognized that spirit in him." I was so young and naive, I thought I was grown and knew him better than my mother. I remember saying to my mom "You have to get to know him better, mom he is so nice." Not knowing that my mom had seen something in him that was familiar from her own past. I didn't know that my mom was giving me advice from a place that she had experienced in her own life, which gave her the signs, the insight, and the wisdom to see what I had was nothing less than trouble that I was not ready for.

I thought it was love because he was always calling and chasing after me, buying nice things, and taking me out on the best dates. Telling me that I was the best girlfriend he had ever had; me being immature, not knowing the difference between real or fake love. I was thinking because he was always buying me such beautiful things, but he knew the type of young lady I was, used to having nice things. My mother made sure our needs were met, she made sure that we didn't want for anything. So, he knew his game had better be tight in that area.

Thinking I knew better, I decided I was going to prove to my mother that she was wrong about him. Show her that this man not only loved me, but he was going to treat me like the queen she raised me to be. So, I continued my relationship with him.

Later I found out that I was expecting, we both were so excited. He asked me to marry him, and I said yes. He gave me a beautiful ring to seal the deal. Everything seemed to be going great, I was so happy that we were going to raise our child together, married and as a family.

Shortly after the news of me expecting our first child, he was offered a promotion, but it came with him moving to another state across the country. So, he accepted the promotion and we relocated to another state together. Nevertheless, that did not change our plans of getting married after our baby was born.

Once we relocated, we found a beautiful place to live. Then came the baby and he was so helpful with our baby he would get up in the morning with the first feeding, as well as change her diaper before he went off to work. On the weekends he would get up early and take our baby for a long walk around the park; giving me some me-time to refresh. At that time, I was not working, I was a stay-at-home mom by his decision, and he was the sole provider of our family. I tell you I had it made or at least I thought I did. Everything seemed to be going well.

Thank God for Prophecy ...

I could not go anywhere without running into a Christian that prophesied to me about the very thing my mother said to me concerning this man not being the will of God for me. God was always giving me warnings that regardless of what I would go through with this man, that I was going to make it out alive. "No weapon that is formed against me shall prosper." Isaiah 54:17

Right before I left Buffalo, I went to my mom and bonus dad church because they were in a revival. The guest minister called me up and prophesied to me about the sex of my baby, and he was right. He also said that "I was going to move to Los Angeles." Now I was in such disbelief because we were leaving the next day to relocate to Seattle Washington. I did not know at that time that later we would end up in Los Angeles. This minister went on to say, "That I was going to be treated like a dog by the man I was with." Now you can just about imagine how I felt, I didn't want to leave with him. I had changed my mind to stay in Buffalo, with all the thoughts running through my mind of what was just spoken to me by the man of God. Of course, expecting my first baby, I didn't want to raise my baby as a single parent along with his pleading with me to leave with him; I continued with my original plans and left with him. I ignored all that was just spoken to me.

No sooner than relocating to Seattle, I remember one day being in the mall. and I saw a young lady about my age, who's hair looked so beautiful and healthy. I approached her and asked her who did her hair. She gave me the name and the telephone number of the salon she went to, so I called and booked an appointment immediately. As soon as I walked into the salon, the stylist asked me, "Was I a Christian before?" I answered her "Yes I was," She, said "The man that I was with is very controlling and mean," she continues to say, "he was going to take me through, but when it was all over because of the call of God on my life and the prayers over me, that I was going to make it out alive." I remember leaving her salon thinking at that time, is this some type of conspiracy about my happiness? I said, "I will never go back to that salon again," even though I was very pleased with my hair. At that time I hadn't seen any signs of what she had said to me.

Some time had passed and I noticed how slowly he started to change. He would build me up, to only tear me down. People say names never hurt but they do. To me, name calling hurts more than anything, it is so degrading and dehumanizing. In time, depending on the severity of the physical pain, one can forget how it felt to be hit, because eventually your body heals. However, mental abuse targets your memory, your mind, and your self-esteem. You continue to keep a list of all the negative things that were said to you, that's abuse in your mind. Mental abuse also affects your self-image and your self-worth.

Then the disagreeing, we could not agree on anything. Then the constant mood swings that led to the fighting. It started occasionally once a month, then it progressed to every little thing that went wrong in his life. From the things he could not control, I now had to pay the price for it. I was blamed for everything, his lack of success, his lack of control, it was always my fault for making him beat me up. Really! By this time the wedding plans were placed on hold by me, until I saw some changes for the better in him.

The abuse got worse and he became more controlling, emotionally, and physically abusive to me. I thought he was so in love with me. I had to find out later that he was a man who had a past full of pain and hurt from his family. An old saying says "hurting people hurts other people." I learned this the hard way, that everything that looks good is not good.

As I began to soul search, asking myself how did I get here? I had to start from the beginning on how he came into my life. How he acted like he was my knight and shining armor, everyone except for my mother thought he was such a nice guy. You know they have a way of showing their best side, too much charm only covers up their evil.

I went through a time where I kept feeling like it was all my fault that he beat me up. Thinking that maybe I should not have said that or did that or spent this. Because I never saw abuse in my home, I didn't know the signs. So, I continued to change myself until I realized that the problem was not me at all; but him.

Shortly, those words that the stylist prophesied to me, had come right back in my face. When he first hit me, I wanted to believe that would be the only time. But it wasn't, it kept getting worse. To the point of what the minister at the revival in my hometown, and the lady at the salon said to me came true. Those very words came right back to me, on how I was going to be treated. "That I was going to make it out alive." Those words I held on to for dear life because at that time I hadn't a clue how to get out.

It had gotten so bad that it did not matter where we were or who we were around, in public places or in the privacy of our home, this man always wanted to FIGHT! I just could not take it anymore. I got so sick and tired of the "I'm sorry' s," until the next fight and the gifts of guilt that followed behind the fighting.

I knew I deserved better than this, and this was not the end of my story because of the prophecy that was spoken over my life; "that I was going to make it out alive." That gave me hope, that regardless of what I was going through he could not kill me. Thank God for His men and women of God who prophesy the Word of God.

The Plan to Escape...

I was so disappointed in myself that I allowed anyone to treat me like that, and that I went against everything I was taught to be with this man. This is what happens when you look for love in all the wrong places and date someone who is unequally yoked with you, 2 Corinthians 6:14. I knew I had to leave him. I no longer cared about him or raising our daughter together as a family in the same household. I wanted better for my daughter and myself. I wanted out!

As happy as I was of the birth of my one and only beautiful daughter, whom I love so much and thank God for her existence. Having her was the greatest blessing that came out of this relationship. I've always said "my daughter has been better to me than ten sons could have ever been." I did not want to be a single mom because everything that I went through in my childhood without my dad; I now realize that it was better to raise my daughter in a single-family household alone, than to allow her to see things that I never saw in my household as a child, and that is abuse. Now, I'm finding myself in the same familiar place in history in my adult life again. The very thing that I hated growing up without my dad in the home has become our generational curse.

The man I once loved now has become a monster living right in my home. He was filled with so much hatred, anger, and bitterness. The abuse had gotten so bad that I knew if I didn't get away from him, I would end up dead.

Thank God for hearing my cry. I called my mom, and for the first time I explained to her all that I had gone through with this man. She got on the next flight to Los Angeles and flew in the next day where I was, and we both flew back to my hometown Buffalo, where I settled at safety. Thank you, Father God.

I Thought the Storm had Passed...

After returning home to Buffalo, safe and sound, I thought it was over. There was a revival in the city of Buffalo, and my mom and I went to hear a lady Evangelist on one of the nights she was in revival. The night I went to hear the Evangelist, when she got up to minister, she called my mother up and asked my mom "did she have a daughter that is light skinned? My mom answered back and said, "Yes I have a couple of daughters that are light skinned." The Evangelist asked, "Is one of them fairer than them all." My mom answered, "Yes she's right here." The women called me up and began to minister to me. She said, "are you married?" I said "no." She said, "there is a man in your life, I believe he's the father of your child, and she went on to say he is going to try to kill you." I looked at this woman with disgust. I was so upset because I thought I was done with this man. He was living in another state, on the other side of the United States from where I was. I was thinking, Lord, will I ever break free of this man? She also stated that God was going to make a way out for me." Then she laid her hands on me and prayed for God's protection over me. I went back to my seat annoyed and aggravated thinking, this could not be of God.

The following week there was a knock at my apartment door, it was no other than my daughter's father. Not thinking at that time what was just ministered to me in church a week ago from the Evangelist from out of town, I answered the door I asked him. "What are you doing here?" He replied that, "he came to visit his daughter." This was our first time seeing one another after I left him in Los Angeles

I invited him in, when he entered my apartment, from the looks of things, it seemed that I was pretty much settled in. This was now home for me. I placed my daughter in his arms for him to hold her and spend time with her. While he was holding her, he was walking around my apartment. Looking around and getting familiar with where everything was. The more he talked, he appeared to be getting angrier and angrier as his tone grew louder and louder. He said, "Because of me, he had to come so far just to see his only daughter." As we continued talking the nastier, he was getting.

While he was still holding our daughter, he walked into her bedroom and placed her in her crib with some of her toys and shut her bedroom door as he walked out. I asked him "Why did he put her in her crib and close her door?" He said that "He was going to kill me for taking his daughter away from him!"

My heart began to race, everything appeared to be moving so fast. By this time, he had placed something in front of the doorway of the entrance to my apartment, barricading me in. Now, preventing me from getting away. I was trapped inside my own apartment. He turned on the stove where I had some cooking grease, saying, "when it gets hot, I'm going to throw it on you." My mind was all over the place. I didn't know if he was telling the truth or not, but I knew I was not going to wait around to find out. My heart was beating so fast, thinking how I could get away from this man. All I knew is that I had to get me and my daughter out of that house before he hurt us. Unfortunately, every time I tried to get my daughter to leave; he would stop me. Snatching me back by my hair, and taking her out of my arms. He shouted, telling me that, "I was going to pay for leaving him!"

I was terrified of him; he had this look in his eyes that I had never seen before. I didn't know what to do. I thought, should I go for it and run alone? Or stay because I did not want to leave without my baby? I heard my neighbor downstairs in his apartment. Once a second opportunity came, I broke free, and I ran downstairs screaming, kicking, and knocking on his door. He caught me again and dragged me back up the stairs by my hair. I continued to kick, scream, and fight him back while he was dragging me up the stairs. Hoping that my neighbor would hear me, then come to help me or call the police. This man was 6'1 and I'm 5"3, I was no match for him. When he pulled me back into my apartment, I just composed myself and caught my breath. Hoping I could come up with a plan to escape. He made it very difficult for me to leave, by tearing my clothes off and taking my shoes.

That did not stop me from looking for an opportunity to leave, a thought came to me thinking, he may hate me enough to kill me, but do I really believe he would harm his daughter? I wanted to believe that he wouldn't harm her, however at that time I was too afraid to take that chance. So, I waited for another opportunity to come to get me and my daughter out of there. However, that opportunity never came for me to leave with her. While I was sitting on the floor in the kitchen where he held me, I started to pray within my mind "God please help me to get out of here," as he was still beating on me. As hard as it was for me to leave my daughter behind, the only way I could make it out was to make a run for it. I had to run the opposite direction of my daughter's bedroom. I had to leave her behind! I believed that God opened that opportunity for me to take a run for my freedom. I believed He was going to protect and keep my daughter safe until I returned with help.

As soon as he turned his back on me, I took that opportunity again and ran out the upstairs door. I ran down the stairs with hardly any clothes on out the downstairs door. This was part of his ploy to keep me from running. I kept running down the street where I lived, screaming and yelling "help please, somebody help me please." Until someone stopped and helped me.

A Ram in The Bush...

I went screaming and running down the street for anyone to see or hear me. Thank God a taxi driver saw me and pulled over to the curb on the side where I was running. He opened his door and shouted "hurry get in." He gave me something to cover myself up with and asked me "Are you okay?" I told him "No!" I explained to him that "My ex-boyfriend had just beaten me up," and that he was threatening to kill me. I continued to explain to the driver that my ex was boiling cooking grease on my stove to throw on me, but I got away. I told him that my baby was still in the apartment. I had to leave her because he wouldn't let me get to her." At this time the taxi driver called on his dispatch for help.

Now, while he was on dispatch calling for assistance for the police to be sent to my address, who would have thought that at the very same time, my very own brother would be in a taxicab by the same company. When my brother heard the address over the radio dispatch, he told his driver to take him to that address that was just announced over the radio dispatch he said, "That is my sister's address!"

Nobody but God. Upon my brother's arrival, 'Boy," I was so happy to see someone from my family, yes, my one and only brother came to my rescue. He immediately took his coat off himself and he covered me with his coat and wrapped his arms around me. This was on one of the coldest, chilliest, snowiest nights in Buffalo.

The SWAT Team, the Police, the News Channels, and Child and Family Service all were called. They were all in front of my apartment. I was so hurt and embarrassed. The reason all the authorities were called was because my daughter's father refused to release our daughter to me; and according to the police officer, my ex had placed our daughter in danger by locking her in a room, and boiling cooking grease on the stove. The officer stated that "if he would have thrown the hot grease on me, the hot grease could have accidentally hit our daughter. Not to mention, it could have caused a fire, and that put our daughter in harm's way."

It seemed like we were waiting outside forever for my ex to surrender. While we were waiting, all types of thoughts were running through my mind. Praying God, please touch his mind to release my daughter and surrender. I just could not believe what I had just experienced. Then, I remembered the Word of God from the Evangelist that was just in town, "that God was going to make a way out for me;" and He did. So, I had to trust that God would cover my daughter as well, and "that no harm shall come nigh thee." No sooner than those thoughts came to me, my ex surrendered with our daughter. She was placed safely back into my arms by Child and Family Services, Praise God.

The Brokenness from Abuse ...

After going through that abusive relationship, my self-esteem hit rock bottom. I was in a state of depression for years. I hated to go places because I was always thinking that everyone was looking at me and laughing at me, because I allowed this man to treat me like that. Thinking that everyone knew what I had been through, the beatings, the name calling, being treated like a dog, from a man who claimed to love me. I never felt so low in my life. I could not believe that I didn't pay any attention to any of the signs. Asking myself "How could I miss the signs?" How did I get here? Beating myself, because I listen to the words of my mother? I kept going over and over in my head, how could I believe that this man ever loved me. When he was so mean to me. Why did I stay so long having him think that what he was doing to me, I was okay with it?

Thinking about all the conversations I shared with him. About how I felt about the absence of my dad not being there, for him not validating me and how that hurt me. All the broken promises he made to me, how he would never hurt me, or our daughter. He promised that he would always be there to protect us, love us and take care of our daughter. How could you say those words and do those mean and evil things to me? That is not love but self-hate!

Thinking how foolish I was to accept his ring to marry him; because I thought he loved me. I was so angry at myself but even more disappointed for not listening to my mother. No man that loves you would put his hands on you to beat you; only to love you. One thing for sure, I was so happy that I never married him, that I continued to push the date back, waiting for him to change. This was the best thing that I could have not done with this man! It was OVER!

One thing I knew was that I did not want him in my life anymore. I'd rather be alone and raise my daughter alone as a single mom, than stay with a man that beat on me. All forms of abuse are degrading. It is not worth anyone staying in a relationship with, rather it is verbal, physical, or mental. It all leaves deep scars.

During those times in my life, we didn't talk about abuse or mental disease like we do now, we didn't have Lifetime Movies to help us understand the dynamics of abuse. I remember my first time watching a Lifetime Movie, I wanted to scream out loud and say, "this was my life?" I didn't talk about it because I was too afraid of being judged or ridiculed because of the lack of knowledge and understanding from others on abuse, in the church as well as in the world. Most of my friends never knew the abuse that I suffered because it was too difficult to talk about with them. When I would talk about it, I was tired of hearing "I can't believe you allowed that to happen" or "How strong I was." As if strong people don't have feelings. Like I always said, "strong people are made, not born." Abuse has no certain look, you can be beautiful, smart, intelligent, well-groomed, wealthy, or poor. When you get involved with a sick, hurting, and abusive person you become their target, their victim without your permission. Thank God for the freedom that we can talk about abuse now, and not be victimized all over again. Thank God for the information and help that is made available for us today.

I encourage anyone who is in an abusive relationship, to tell someone to get help, and most importantly to get out of it safely. You deserve so much better than that. I never thought I would be in such a violent, dehumanizing, degrading relationship in my life; that was the worst thing I had ever experienced.

If you are in a Domestic Violence Relationship, there is help available for you. **National Domestic Hotline (800) 799-7233**

Part 3

The Beginning of My Restoration

I was so emotionally and mentally messed up, the only one who could fix me was God. I needed my mind to be restored; I would cry out to God ``help me!'' Thank God for the Word of God because there is healing in the Word of God.

I rededicated my life back to God. I never knew how much being in that relationship had taken a toll on my mind, body, and soul, until I was out of the mental bondage that relationship had held over me for years. I remember feeling so afraid, paralyzed, and mentally exhausted to do anything, all I wanted to do was stay in my apartment away from everyone and sleep all day.

I thank God for a praying mother and the prayers that were prayed over my life, that's what helped me. "For the prayers of the righteous avail it much," James 5:16. One thing I learned from that experience is that whatever I go through, I learned to take it to God in prayer. It does not matter what the situation may be, I learned to give it to God. I began to seek after God and all His righteousness like I never sought after him before. My mind was being set free from the negative thoughts that tried to keep me in bondage. During that time, I remember that I could not get enough of talking to (the Lord). Often, I thought I was becoming too spiritual, good, and no earthly good (lol.) All I wanted to do was pray and talk to the Father, that's where I felt safe. There were many times I couldn't wait to get in the privacy of my home, to tell my Heavenly Father how my day was. As soon as I would enter my apartment I would say, "Hi Father. I couldn't wait to come home and talk with you." Even as I am writing this part in the book, I have the biggest smile on my face because it feels so good to be loved by the greatest love of all, God.

I tell you I got hooked on the Lord. The more I sought after Him the more I was being set free and I loved every moment of it.

This is where I learned who I was to God and how much he loves me, and that there was "nothing that could separate me from the love of God," Romans 8:38. This became a testament in my life, because as I read, I began to see God for who He really was. **Mighty!**

I remember times in my prayer time, hearing the spirit of the Lord saying such beautiful, sweet, kind, and loving words to me. "Oh, taste and see that the LORD is good." Psalm 34:8 I started keeping a journal, writing everything down that was spoken to me in my prayer time, every promise that God made to me. Every word that was spoken to me from the women and men of God. "I wrote it down. "Write the vision, make it plain." Habakkuk 2:2.

One of my favorite things I loved was after the Holy Spirit would give me something in my spirit in my private prayer time, I would go to the bible, open right to a scripture that confirmed just what I heard in my prayer time from the Lord.

I have seen the hand of God move mightily in my life. I look back and see all that God has brought me through, I can't help but say "If it had not been for the Lord that was on my side." Psalm 124:2

Nobody but God does that!

The Power of Prayer...

In His presence there is" peace that passes all understanding," Philippians 4:7. I tell you it came a time that all I did was pray to stay in the presence of God, in His presence is healing and liberty. I no longer felt ashamed as a victim, because I had victory in my life. Every time God would give me the opportunity to share my story with others, I did. There is freedom in telling others where you've been. They are encouraged to know that "God is not a respecter of person." Romans 2:11 What he did for me He will do for you.

Money can't buy this type of peace, or joy only in His presence. In my prayer time, God would give me the plan for my life, on how he was going to restore, renew, and revive everything that was taken from me. Joel 2:25.

In my prayer is where I learned about who God was and why I was created. I began to denounce the negative demonic words of the devil and replaced what the word of God said about me. Some may say, it doesn't take all this to be free. I'm here to say whatever it takes, I wanted to be free to live the life God planned for me.

When you pray God will show you the hidden treasures of your life. Isaiah 45:3-25 At one time in my life, I was so busy looking at all the weeds that had surrounded me in that abusive relationship, instead of the one beautiful rose, right in the midst of the weeds. Yes, my greatest blessing God has granted me was to be a mom. I took that job more seriously than any job I ever had in my entire life, regardless of what I had to go through. I loved being a mom. I read the word of God, that children are a gift from God. Psalm 127:3 So, whether I had to raise my beautiful daughter as a single mom, she was mine to love, nurture, cover, and protect according to the plan of God. As I continued in my life as a single parent, I started seeing things about myself that I would have never seen, had I not been a single parent. Being a parent, I wanted to be the best mom and best role model in my daughter's life. I also wanted to teach her the beauty of loving who she is. I wanted to be the best that I could be, so I had to let God continue to work within me. My daughter is grown up now, and I could not be prouder of the woman that she has become

To God be the Glory. Whatever I go through to this day, I give it to God in prayer until I see a change. "Do not be anxious about anything, but in everything, by prayer and petition, with thanksgiving, present your request to God." Philippians 4:6,7:

"So, I say to you: Ask and it will be given to you; seek and you will find; knock and the door will be opened to you. For everyone who asks receives; he who seeks finds; and to him who knocks, the door will be opened." Luke 11:9-13: Therefore, it is so important to have a prayer life.

Behold I Will Do A New Thing...

Behold, I will do a new thing; now it shall spring forth; shall ye not know it? I will even make a way in the wilderness, and rivers in the desert. Isaiah 43:19. God did a new thing in me.

God taught me how to encourage and affirm myself. I began to walk in assurance, knowing that there were no greater words of affirmation, than the Word of God. The power of darkness has been broken over me. Now, only God's Word, and His thoughts are the only opinion of me that matters. I would look into the mirror while I was preparing myself to leave my home, and I would say these words to myself, "Michelle you are fearfully and wonderfully made. Girl there is no one like you, God loves you so much, you are the apple of His eye." I would say these words of affirmation with conviction and attitude. The more I began to speak God's Word to myself, my head would raise, my shoulder would roll back, and the biggest smile of confidence would appear on my face. I had an attitude to my walk. You have to agree and believe with what the Word of God says about you. The more I would repeat these affirmations to myself in the mirror, I began to see a change in myself. "Whose report are you going to believe? I will believe in the report of the Lord."

My confidence was lifted because of the word of God, it silences all the voices of darkness in my head. Isn't God good?

A Ministry Birth...

I began to learn that "I can do all things through Christ who strengthens me." Philippians 4:13 "If God be for me who can be against me." Romans 8:31 Those things that I once felt so inadequate about myself and thought they were so farfetched for me to reach. I was able to conquer them all with the help of God.

When I knew I was free from the bondage of abuse and low self-esteem, I wanted to teach every young lady that I met. That having a healthy self-esteem is the will of God.

Charm & Etiquette with Michelle charm school was born. A School for young ladies, teaching young ladies' charm and etiquette from the ages 8 to 16 years old. Teaching them who they are and how precious they are to God. "Train up a child in the way he should go and when he is old, he will not depart from it." Proverbs 22:6 Teaching them the beauty of loving who God created them to be and empowering them that they can "do all things through Christ." Training them how to appreciate their self-worth and their value, even if your birth father never told you who you are, God left a blueprint in His Word (The Bible) a clear description of who you are. I want every young person to know how great they are. An African Proverb say" It takes a village to raise a child." This became my guiding tool in life, and this is my part in the village, teaching other family's daughters to love who God created them to be. To walk in acceptance of knowing everything that God created is good. Rather you are big, small, thin, tall, short, light, medium or dark, you have a God given right to love who you are. God created you just the way you are for His perfect plan that He has just for you.

I teach young ladies to this day to look in the mirror and tell themself who they are and how beautiful they are. Validate yourself first and when others do, it will only be a compliment **and** not a stamp of validation or approval. It won't alter what you think of yourself one way or another. The only opinion that should matter is yours and God's.

Too many times we look for others to tell us who we are, and when their opinion changes about us we get messed up. That's too much power for anyone to have over you. Stop allowing all these fake images, people, television, magazine ads and all these reality shows etc.; alter the way you think or feel about yourselves and go straight to the Creator who created you. Stop allowing the world to dictate to you that you must look a certain way in order to be loved, that is so far from the truth.

I begin every class by teaching my students to look in the mirror in front of their classmates and validate themselves. Yes, every one of them has felt a little strange talking to themselves in the mirror in front of their peers but once you start believing in what you are saying, that strange feeling does leave. My grandmother used to say, "You are Feeling yourself." Everyone needs to have a high self-esteem, just to face this world that has so many descriptions of who you should be.

Try looking in the mirror and affirm yourself, you will love it. As you look in the mirror start with telling yourself "I am beautiful, I am fearfully and wonderfully made," I can do all things through Christ who strengthens me." Before you're done, God will open your eyes to see the beauty that you behold and how unique you are, and why you were created to be different from everyone else. He will show you your qualities, that you may have been told you had, but you never saw in yourself. Because of the things the devil whispered in your ear. The more you speak God's Word to yourself, the more you will see that God created you for greater things, you are more than just your physical beauty. When you start to see that you are unstoppable, you're precious; you were created in the image of God and everything He created is good!

I Said Yes to The Call...

I ran so many years from the call, I got tired of running and said," Yes to the Lord". One thing I learned is that when I surrender it's so much easier, because He will get the glory out of your life sooner or later, that depends on you. "The blessing of the LORD, MAKES it rich, and He adds no sorrow." Proverbs 10:22 That's when we walk in His will.

God has an expected end for you. "For I know the plans I have for you," declares the LORD, "plans to prosper you and not to harm you, plans to give you hope and a future." Jeremiah 29:11

When I accepted the call of God in my life, life got better. From studying the word of God, I received my license as an Evangelist of the Gospel, what a joyous accomplishment this was for me. Being in ministry was one of the things that I loved doing the most. Whether it was cleaning the church bathrooms, teaching our youth bible study, or speaking to others about the goodness of God, I loved doing whatever I could set my hands to do.

Do everything unto God because He's the one that sees it all and He is your rewarder. I remember while cleaning the church, it gave me the opportunity to pray for the church and set the tone of worship before the people came. While I clean, I would pray that God's presence would fill that place. I learned that cleaning the church was just as important as every other job in the church. I wanted my heavenly Father to see me cleaning, like I cleaned my home, spotless to perfection! There was nothing too good for my Heavenly Father. Never take for granted what you do for the Father when you do it unto God. I learned that nothing goes unseen by God. God will open doors for you that no man can open, just because of your faithfulness and willingness to please the Father more than man. Regardless if you are a cook, cleaner, singer, preacher, or an usher, be faithful with it, do your best unto God. Know that all gifts and talents belong to God for the body of Christ.

It's never about you, but it's all about the plan of God. He will take whatever you've been through and get the glory out of it. God will use your past, your hurts, your brokenness, your mishaps, your misfortune, your disability, your marriage, your divorce, your loss, your success, and your blessings to help someone else to break free.

In sharing your truth with others who are presently where you once were, it gives them hope in God, that there is deliverance for them. "Trust and hope in God! I know God's plan for me was to help other women and young ladies who have been where I once was, to speak a word of hope in their present situation, to deliver them out of their low places of darkness and know who they are to Jesus Christ. I am doing what I was created to do.

Part 4

Living Single and Whole

Too often **as** a single woman, we are so busy waiting for Mr. Right that time slips right by us and the result is time wasted. I believe that God wants us to enjoy and live our best lives while we are single as well. We spend too much time and money preparing for the wedding day and not enough time on ourselves. Get to know you before you invite someone else into your life.

Finding your mate is not your job, but the responsibility of the man to find you. "² Whoso finds a wife finds a good thing and he obtained favor of the LORD." Proverbs 18:22 This means you are the favor, the blessing from the Lord, and it also means that for your mate to find you. Now in order for him to find you, he must have a relationship with God; so that he can get instructions on where to find you or when he does find you, to know that you are his "bone of his bone and flesh of his flesh."

Genesis 2:23 It's not about being in a race or competition with other women to see who marries first. As women we should always celebrate and keep each other lifted and encouraged, regardless of our marital status. If your desire is to be married, stay encouraged that God will give you the desires of your heart, just as he has done for so many others.

Being single is not a sign of being inadequate, unwanted, or incomplete. **Because we all started at the same place "Single." So, tell that demon from the pit of hell to get behind you!** Know that your time for marriage just has not come yet, so for that reason it just takes some of us a little longer. "For everything there is a season, and a time for every purpose under heaven:" Ecclesiastes 3:1-8

In the meanwhile, while you wait you continue to stay encouraged, and continue to love you. Live your best life as a single person who God has made whole and complete. The bible says, "the two shall become one flesh;" Mark 10:8. This means two whole people become one flesh, the soul tie, the connection takes place in your soul; by the two souls knitted together spiritually.

So, don't worry about being single, or when the husband will come, I learned that if God doesn't send him, he won't be sent. God has taught me to be happy in whatever state I'm in. Philippians 4:11-14. I look at all my blessings that God so graciously granted me. I know for sure regardless of my marital status or what comes or goes, that I was given a responsibility to share the good news to others about the greatness of God.

I remember one time I was asked to speak at a single's conference. When I was told the format of the program and what was expected of me to speak on, I kindly declined; the Topic was "Preparing for the Wedding Day." This is a great topic for the women who are already engaged to be married and know who their mate is. But not for a woman who does not have a clue who her mate is and doesn't have a ring of commitment, which was me. I don't believe in buying items or trinkets for a wedding day before you meet your mate. That is not faith to me, that is a waste of time, and money. Furthermore, shouldn't your future husband have something to say about his wedding day as well? Don't start a relationship based on only what you want, when it takes two to marry, so the two of you both have dreams and desires that should matter. It's his day as well as yours.

Single women in your time of preparation get your mind, body, and spirit right for your Mr. Right. You should get your **Mind** right by knowing your worth as a single person first before you could ever know who YOU are with someone else. **Body** -love your body, and if you want to make changes to it, then do so because you want to; be happy with all of you first before you can expect someone else to be happy with you. **Spirit**- get your spirit right with the Creator because God created mankind in his own image, "in the image of God he created them; male and female he created them." Genesis 1:27. God is the blueprint to your life. "Seek first the kingdom of God and his righteousness, and all these things will be added to you. "Matthew 6:33 Live your best life and be blessed and encouraged; God has your perfect mate just for you.

I have so many responsibilities that I'm still trying to perfect. One of them is being the best daughter, sister, mom, nana, CEO of Charm & Etiquette with Michelle Charm School, mentor, Christian, and furry mommy (to my dog, Baby Bear). If I never have the title of "wife" please know my life is full and I am blessed. Not being a wife does not deplete me of who I am to myself or to so many others; Know who you are and continue to walk with your head lifted high and know that you are a special gem that God our Father created. So, ladies shine and don't let a title or position dim your light.

One Mother's Day Night...

I was in a place in my life that I loved more than anything, and that was doing ministry. God was opening doors for me and I was happy about it and happy to do what I was called to do. One of the things I loved about ministry was how the Lord used me. At this time in my life, I had lost over 35 pounds and had just had some work done on my teeth. I met a handsome man of God who I was attached to. Ladies, life was good! I loved where I was in my life at that time. But the unforeseen happened.

I was in a horrible car accident on Mother's Day night in 2009 and that changed everything or at least I thought it did. I had just left my mother's house celebrating her for being the best mother to me. All my mother's children and their spouses, her grandkids, and her great grandkids, all went to one of Buffalo's finest restaurants to celebrate. Traditionally, after dinner everyone met at one of my family members' houses for dessert and coffee. That Mother's Day we all went over to my mother's house for dessert and coffee. We are a Christian family; my mother and my bonus dad are pastors of the church that I attend to this day; my brother and his wife are leaders as well. The television was on the christian channel. I will never forget his message, the minister on the television said, "God was setting a table in the presence of my enemies. That Word seems like God was speaking to me." Psalm 23:4-6. I got so excited about the table of blessings, that I never thought about the valley part.

The accident in 2009...

It was getting late, and everyone was leaving because some had to work the following morning. Normally I would have stayed the night over to my parents house because I was single and lived alone. However, my daughter had left her car at my place because we had driven together. So, my beautiful daughter who was expecting her second child at the time, and my granddaughter who was five years old at that time, was with us as well.

When my daughter got to the car, she placed my precious granddaughter in her car seat and fastened her in. Then, she got into the front passenger seat of the car and fastened herself in. So, after we were all seated and fastened in I said to my daughter, clowning around, "sit back and relax, I got this." At that time, I put on my stereo and put in one of my favorite gospel CD's. I remember the song that I played was ("Trusting in you Lord). Then, we headed on to my place where my daughter had left her car.

Now, this was a route that I had always taken home from visiting my mother's house for years. I would go and see my mother at least four times out of a week. So, I was very familiar with this area, not to mention that I was only five minutes away from home.

As I was getting off my exit on the 33, Buffalo's Expressway and entering regular traffic; a car came driving so fast that I didn't even see it coming. According to the police report the driver was intoxicated and high on narcotics, and she failed to stop at a stop sign which caused her to T-bone me. She hit my car at the front door of the driver's side. My car was hit so hard that it was completely totaled; all airbags deployed. My grandbaby was locked down in a car seat, but we were hit so hard that her car seat went completely underneath the front seat on the passenger's side. I was fastened in my seat with my seatbelt on and because of the impact, I was knocked completely into the passenger's seat from the driver's seat, right into my pregnant daughter's lap and passed out.

The Angel of The Lord Appeared ...

Now during this time, I was still unconscious, but I remember thinking that the car was going to catch on fire or explode and I needed to get us out. However, every time in my mind I tried to move, I couldn't. I was trapped in my car. I remember seeing myself screaming from the pain that I was in. I heard my daughter say, "Mom please don't move," then I saw this man come out of nowhere and lift me up and out of my car. He got me out, and he carried me to safety. Now, let me take a pause for just a moment to say that I had lost some weight, however, the way this man had cradled me was like I was as small as a baby, because that's what I had seen while I was unconscious. He had to have some type of supernatural strength to carry me like that. While he was carrying me, he whispered in my ear and said, "Trust in the Lord with all your heart." Then he laid me down on the grass between the walkway and the curb and then he walked away.

To this day, no one knows who this man was, or where he came from or where he went to. Others who witnessed the accident also saw this man carrying me and placing me on the grass. In the police report, it states "Unidentified man got the victim (me) out of the car and carried the victim (me) to safety." Even my daughter says that "she went to thank him, and it was like he had disappeared." I believe to this day that was an angel of the Lord.

The next thing I remember was seeing my body being placed in the ambulance and all these things were being done to me to save my life. An IV was being put into my arm, then I saw a defibrillator was being used on me. I can hear the workers in the ambulance say, "we are losing her." I see them placing these defibrillators on my chest and I heard someone say, "clear." All of this took place while I was in the ambulance. I don't remember if the car was moving or not, I do remember that during all this turmoil, I was still unconscious.

While I Was Unconscious...

I was taken to the emergency room at Erie County Medical Center, ECMC, one of Buffalo's best Hospitals known for their trauma unit, because of my head injuries. When I arrived at the hospital, I was still unconscious, but I remember seeing everything that was going on. I saw all my clothes being cut off and I was able to hear all the conversations that were going on while I was being treated. How pretty my makeup was and how pretty my undergarments were. Remember when your grandmother used to tell you to always wear nice undergarments because you just never know? Well, I can truly thank her for that. I saw a machine that appeared to be like a clear vacuum that was sucking the glass and my broken teeth out of my mouth. The front windshield had shattered, and most of the glass went into my face and my mouth. There was so much glass that went into my body that for months, every time I would blow my nose or cough, a piece of glass would come up and out.

I saw my brother who is the eldest of all five of us, and my eldest sister standing in the room with me while I was being treated. Both were crying and appeared to be taking it very hard. I had never seen them like this before. My eldest sister was hitting her right fist into her left hand repeatedly saying "Darn, darn." While my brother was looking with tears running down his face.

The doctors told my family that "it does not look good and that I may not make it through the night," so they were very lenient on allowing my immediate family members to come in and see me. At that time, I had seen all my family members one by one. My brother, sisters, my bonus dad, nieces, nephews, and the Pastor and Elders from Bethesda Full Gospel Church. I saw everyone except my daughter pass away? I thought my daughter and granddaughter didn't survive the car accident. I also thought where is my mom?

The Visions...

After seeing all my family members at the hospital that night I thought I had transitioned to what I believe was heaven, yes, I thought I had passed away as well. In this part of the vision, I saw myself running, I mean I was running so fast because I was so excited to make it to that place I believed was heaven. I was running so fast with high heel shoes on, one would think that I would have fallen or slipped because I was running so fast.

This place looked so mystical and beautiful with a long hallway that led to an entrance to a door that was closed, and the door looked as if it was pure gold. It was a beautiful place that I had never seen before. This area was so bright and lit up with the most brilliance of lighting, but I did not see any light fixtures. However, the area that I was in was lit with the brightest light. The floors appeared to be so shining, beautiful like crystal glass that sparkled like diamonds; they sparkled better than the finest Waterford Crystal that I had ever seen. I also saw tall huge walls that I could not see over. Towering in front of them were huge, enormous size, gorgeous angels with pure white massive feathers extending from their backs, standing in position as if they were on guard. I'm not certain if they were even looking at me while I was running up to what I believed was the hallway to an entrance in heaven; I do know that these angels never said one word to me.

While I was running, I was looking at myself and I was laughing out loud with joy saying "Wow, I beat that car accident." Because while I was running, it appeared that nothing was wrong with me. I had no cuts or open wounds and from the looks of the car accident, there was no way I should have looked as good as I did.

Then all the sudden I heard this voice and it sounded like it was hovering like a surround sound. It was a loud, powerful, strong, authoritative voice, but also sounded very kind and loving saying, "You can't come any further, you must go back, I'm not through with you yet." I begin to cry and plead with who I believe was God and say, "Why Lord, there's no way I could have made it through that accident, there's no way." Then I heard the same voice say to me, "Trust in the Lord with all your heart and lean not unto thine own understanding." Proverbs 3:5.

Then my eyes opened, and the only people that were in the room with me at that time were my eldest sister and my only brother. My eyes closed again, and I went to this place that was so peaceful and tranquil. While I was in this place, I had another vision. I saw my birth father and I lying side by side with our hands behind our heads on top of the hood of an older model car, laughing and talking while we watched the stars in the sky. Then It was like I was floating on this cloud. I was in a place of peace and tranquility, then I went into a deep sleep.

When I came out of the coma, I was told by my doctors that "They didn't think I was going to make it through the first night." I was told that I had suffered a concussion, nine broken ribs, fractured jaw, fractured trachea bone (that's the bone right in the middle of your throat), my lower back, neck injuries, and I suffered pelvic injuries. I was unable to walk, and the entire left side of my body was so dark that it looked as though I was burned. That was from all the bruising and the blood clotting that came from the impact of the SUV hitting me. I was unable to eat solid foods for a year, so I had to have my food puree and be fed like a baby. Besides the physical injuries I endured, memory loss because of my head injury. Everyone that visited me at the hospital was told not to show me a mirror because they didn't want me to see how bad I looked and upset me while I was in recovery.

Part 5

Whose Report Do You Believe

Due to my injuries, I was treated by several different doctors during my years of recovery. A chiropractor for my back injury, otolaryngologist for my throat injury, a neurologist for my head injuries, an oral and maxillofacial surgeon for my jaw replacement, a dentist for my teeth, a medical doctor for the broken bones and bruised ribs/lungs. Finally, a speech therapist I had to relearn how to speak and pronounce certain words. When I was released from the hospital, I had three to five doctor appointments per week for several years. At one time, there was never any good news when I would leave my doctor's appointments, but my trust and hope was in God. I never let go of the words that God had spoken to me while I was unconscious. "Trust in the Lord with all your heart." Proverbs 3:5, I tell you that it is not easy when everyone is telling you differently, but I had no other choice but to trust in God. The doctors had done all that they could do; the rest was in God's hands.

I remember times when I would leave my doctor's appointment and was told that "I would never walk again without some type of assistance," like a walker or a cane. "I will never be able to have teeth replacement, because the bone was destroyed and replaced with titanium plates." I will never forget the one time after being released from the hospital, I was left alone in my apartment for a couple of hours, because my granddaughter had been taken to the hospital because of her asthma. As soon as my daughter left, I remember rolling on the floor and dragging my body to my closet because my legs had not yet gained their strength for me to walk. It was a struggle, but I put on a pair of my shoes and tried to stand up in them. I fell every time, but I never gave up on trusting in God.

Another time comes to mind when I was told that I would not be able to remember things, due to the lack of oxygen I lost from my head injury. I would be in conversation and forget the correct word to use and just pause in thought. I got myself a speaking dictionary and my Bible, and I read the Word of God as difficult as it was for me, I did it anyway. I was determined that this was not going to be how my story ends. I said to myself, "whose report Michelle will you believe?" I would shout out to the rooftop "I will BELIEVE in the report of the Lord!" "Jesus has given us authority over the power of the enemy, and nothing shall in any way harm us; Luke 10:17-19."

Let God be true and every man a liar. "Whose report shall you believe? I shall believe the report of the Lord." When I was told that I would have a problem remembering things, I went back to college and as many times I wanted to quit because of my feelings of inadequacy, I stayed my course; and in my first semester of study, I got a 4.0 average. Nobody but God! Later I received two degrees and graduated with a 3.5 average; I tell you there is nothing you can't do when God the Father says yes!

I thank God for the people that He sent in my life to pray, cheer, and encourage me to do the things that seemed so impossible. Like I always say to my daughter, "God always gives us what we need."

Life can take you down some difficult roads. "Boy," some of those roads have not always been easy, pleasant, or happy, but nevertheless, they were roads that were purposed for me, to bring me to this place in my life today. Happy and full of joy to see the Word of God working in my life. When you are in the well of the Father, everything works out for your good. So, my advice is to live happily regardless of what state you're in. Often you must live for the moment, and like I always tell my daughter, create memories with the people you love because memories are priceless. Create your own happiness because you were only given one life. Stop waiting for someone else to make you happy; that is too big of a responsibility for anyone. Treat yourself good and on your worst days look even better, never let the enemy know your ups or your downs so he won't be able to tell the difference. You feel better when you look good. Validate yourself and most importantly stay connected to the one and only God. Don't allow life's storms to minimize how you feel about your creator, God.

The Reveal ...

After a year of being off from work due to my injuries, I returned to work; much to my doctor's disagreement. My doctor did not want to release me to go back as soon as I did, but I insisted on returning; the result, he released me to return. On my first day back, upon entering my place of work, the love that was awaiting me at my desk was overwhelming. All my co-workers had seen the accident on the news, and they were expecting me to look differently than I did. While I was hospitalized there were some restrictions on visits, so they didn't know what to expect upon my arrival on my first day of return. I walked in wearing this beautiful grey pants suit that my eldest sister gave me with my high heels on. I strutted to my desk with no pain and the biggest smile on my face.

Everyone was standing around me in amazement at how great I looked and that I was walking in my high heels, like they know me to do. There were flowers waiting at my desk, given to me by the director of our company welcoming me back. It was so crowded at my desk that the director of our company had to tell everyone, "I know we all love Michelle and are happy to see her back, but you all have five minutes, then I will need you all to return back to your area." Everyone was in shock at how I did not look like what I had been through. To God be the glory.

I was so overwhelmed that when everyone left my area, I asked to be excused to gather myself. I went to my secret place on the third floor where I would go sometimes to pray and just cry out to God. While I was in my secret place at work, it was when I walked into the room and looked in the mirror, that's when it all came to me. That place in the vision, that I believed was heaven, where I was running with my high heels on looking at myself saying "I beat that car accident." I looked identical to the person I had seen in the vision. I began to just cry out and praise God, because then I knew that God the Father had shown me from the very beginning that I was coming out; and when I came out, I was going to look as if I never went through the storm. Nobody but God can do this.

Some people will never pick up a Bible or go to church. God will use the very thing that looks like there is no hope in your life, and turn it around for your good. For others to see that He is real, He still does specialize in miracles and that He is the same God today that He was back in the bible days, and will be forever more. If it had not been for the LORD who was on my side Psalm 124:1. I tell you I know that it was God working through the doctors, the nurses, the emergency medical technicians and through the man who carried me out of the car. It was all in His plan. Trust and hope in God!

Every Little Girl Needs Her Dad...

A father plays a very intricate role in the family circle, not to mention that he is part of his children's identity and the plan of God. A father is the first man to validate, affirm and place his stamp of approval on his daughter. He protects her, cherishes her, and demonstrates to her the meaning of unconditional love. He's the first example of how a man treats the love of his life, to love her, and never mistreat her, harm her, or abuse her. A father teaches his little girl that the man is the head of the home regardless of who brings home the most money, because this is the order of God. 1 Peter 3:7

Without having a father model these things to his little girl, can cause one to feel like they are not worthy to be loved; and look for love in all the wrong places, trying to fulfill the emptiness that she beholds. When this happens ours, daughters are set up for destruction.

As much as I love my mom and think the world of her, thank God for my mom being my hero. She lacked one thing and that is, she is not my dad. She was not the sole cause of my existence; it takes two. She was only able to teach me from a woman's point of view. We can't ignore the plan and the order of God. There is a purpose for each role as parent or God would have allowed women to be the sole cause of our existence.

My mother taught me how to adore being a young lady, and how to take care of my body. How to act like a lady as well as how to dress appropriately. Like I always say, my mom is the biggest girl ever, she loves and adores being a lady she was the greatest role model. She also taught me how to provide the necessities that I need, and how to cook and keep a clean house. She also taught me right from wrong and how to always walk in forgiveness. She also taught me the Golden Rule, "Do unto others as you would have them do unto you.

Nevertheless, going to school was difficult for me, because all my friends had the very thing that I didn't have, a dad in the home. Being around other children who had both of their parents at home was a constant reminder of what I didn't have. I had this one friend whose house I always went over to visit because I enjoyed seeing the dynamics of her family together, living in the same house, under one roof. I loved watching my friend and her dad and how they acted with one another, how her dad always talked so kindly and sweet to her. When someone would ask where my dad is, I would tell this story, that my dad was always out of town on business trips. It seems like I was always reminded of his absence, it was always in the forefront of my mind, the negative thoughts and lies the devil would speak to me. Often, I could hear the devil's voice louder than my own, that was too big of a burden for any child to carry; but that's what the devil does. These feelings continued in my life until I accepted Jesus Christ into my life as my personal Savior and got to know God as Father through Jesus Christ.

In the black community it is more prevalent for our culture to be raised in a single-family home and raised by one parent. According to statistics children do better when both parents are in the home. Often, when a black man leaves his wife or his children's mother, he walks away from his obligations to his children as well. This was forced on our culture from slavery, black families being separated and torn apart from one another. I just never understood why as a culture, some continue to be separated from their children when we know the damage it does. I'm not just talking about the father's financial responsibility but his appearance, and support emotionally and mentally. When a child is growing up, they need both parents involved in their lives spending time with them more often than few. "Train up a child in the way he should go; even when he is old, he will not depart from it." Proverbs 22:6. "Behold, children are a heritage from the Lord, the fruit of the womb a reward. Like arrows in the hands of a warrior are the children of one's youth. Blessed is the man who fills his quiver with them! He shall not be put to shame when he speaks with his enemies in the gate." Psalm 127:3-5 "Grandchildren are the crown of the aged, and the glory of children is their fathers." Proverbs 17:6

The Great news is when one doesn't have a father in the home to model these things to his little girl, we can go straight to the

Word of God and get a clear understanding on how a Father loves His daughters. Also, how a man treats a woman he loves. The bible says, "that a man takes care of his wife better than he takes care of himself," she should always come first. Ephesians 5:23 The Bible also teaches us that a man leaves his mother and his father and cleaves to his wife. Genesis 2:24 He should never forget that God created her as the weaker vessel in strength only and to never abuse his authority and strength.

Beloved I want to let you know that God never leaves us uncovered, you have a heavenly Father that cares about you and He has you covered! You never have to feel alone or rejected, because your earthly father is not in your life. "He will never leave you or forsake you." Hebrews 13:5. He knows everything about you, "Before you were formed in your mother's womb, He knew you, "Jeremiah 1:5. "Greater love has no one than this: to lay down his own life just for you." John 15:13 "But even the very hairs of your head are all numbered. Fear not therefore: ye are of more value than many sparrows." Luke 12:7.

Most of my youth I walked around thinking I needed to hear all those things from my earthly dad. I wasted so much time not knowing who I was to God the Father, until I gave my life to the Lord and read all those beautiful scriptures in the bible, of how much God loves me. That was all the validation I needed. Even before the Lord called my dad home, my earthly dad spoke into my life. I realized that God was there for me all the time. You see, some of us will never get the validation from our birth parents, because they may have passed on. However, I want to encourage you that you do have a heavenly Father that cares for you. It was never His desire that I felt like that, not being good enough, because everything God created was good!

You are Loved and valued by the greatest Father of all, God.

The Power of DNA...

It was not till years later, literally in my dad's last season, that I learned how powerful the DNA is. This is where I see why I did the things the way I did, and why I reacted to things the way I do. My outspoken personality is so much like my dad's. The power of DNA; the blood line. It wasn't till I went to stay with my father alone to care for him, was when I was able to see a side of me that was missing all my life.

I thank God for filling this emptiness in my life and bringing this full circle. While I was caring for my dad, it was times I would look at him and see my other siblings in him. This was so amazing to me. How powerful the bloodline is? There were times I would look up at him; and catch a glimpse of my brother in the way they walked and talked. Not to mention that they dressed alike and had the same classy style. On one occasion, I was preparing my dad's dinner and he gave me precise instructions on how to cook his steak. I remember walking away laughing, calling him my eldest sister's name (lol) because my eldest sister acts just like him. This was so funny to me. Another time I was in his room oiling his body, when I looked up at him, he looked just like my middle sister. They have the prettiest big brown eyes to me. Then, on another occasion, he was not feeling well. I was very concerned about him, so I explained to him that if he's not feeling better by a certain time, that I was going to take him to the emergency room. He refused and had all of these excuses as to why he didn't need to go to the emergency room. It was something about the way in which he said it, that he sounded and looked just like my youngest sister.

Other times, during different conversations, he would speak right into my heart. I tell you, seeing your identity can cause one to feel so whole and that is powerful! He told me "How beautiful, kind, and sharp I was, and how proud he was of me, and how happy he was that I was there with him at that time." He said that he enjoyed our time together and the conversations that we had. He also spoke about how easy it was to talk to me. He said to me, "I'm so surprised that you are not married Michelle. You would be a great wife." As I explained to him why I never married, it gave me the opportunity to talk to him about his absence from my life. He explained to me "how much he loved my mom and that he will always love her and all their children they have together; but not having his dad in his life really didn't help him on knowing how to be a dad or a husband." He said that "he lived with a lot of hurt, pain, and regret for years, for not being in our lives. He also acknowledged that my mom did a great job raising us all by herself." Tears ran down my face, because I waited a long time to hear those words of validation, affection, and explanation from my dad. All these years had passed and as much as I was angry with my dad, I always loved him so much and just wanted to know that he loved me too.

After hearing all this, I felt so beautiful and loved by my dad. I thought I could do anything because my daddy said I could. Wow, the power of words. I fell so in love with my daddy, I felt like daddy's little girl.

My dad passed away peacefully while I was there taking care of him. As hurt as I was by his death, I was just as grateful to God for allowing me to hear from my earthly dad how much he loved me. I knew God loved me more. Upon returning to my hometown heartbroken, I thought God could have taken my dad before I heard those words from him. Powerful.

Your Change is Coming...

I like to share a story with you to encourage you as it has encouraged me throughout my life. The story is about Joseph; I'm talking about Joseph from "The Coat of Many Colors." I'll make it real short, but the story goes like this:

Joseph was the 12th son of Jacob, and the Bible says that Jacob loved him more than any of his other children, because he had him in his old age, he made him a coat of many colors, Genesis 37:3. Because of Jacob's favoritism towards Joseph, his brothers hated him.

God had given Joseph a dream that one day, his brothers, the moon, and the stars would bow down to him. When Joseph told his brother's the dream, that made them hate him even more. This example teaches us that some people will hate you because of what God has given you concerning your life. For this reason, like my bonus dad used to say to me "Nothing hurts a duck but his bill." This means to stop telling folks everything that you receive in prayer, because the only person it hurts is you. Get you a notebook, a pen and "write it down and make it plain." Habakkuk 2:2

Now his brother's jealousy for him grew, to wanting to kill him, but God said no. So, instead they sold him into slavery, to the traveling caravan of Ishmaelites who took him to Egypt and sold him to Potiphar, the Pharaoh's Captain of the Guard. The Bible says that the Lord's presence was with Joseph, and that he had found favor with Potiphar by interpreting the dreams of the two prisoners, the butler, and baker that came true.

Now Joseph's favor put him in position to interpret a dream of the Pharaoh which was about the seven years of plenty followed by the seven years of famine. Well, because of his God given gift to interpret dreams, Pharaoh promotes Joseph to Chief Administrator of Egypt.

This caused Joseph to have authority over everything that came and went concerning the supplies and demand during those 14 years.

The dream that God gave Joseph came true, about the moon, the stars, and his brothers bowing down to him. It was all in the plan of God for Joseph to be in Egypt at that appointed time, this is how he was purposely placed to preserve the life of his family who lived in the province of Goshen. The rest of this story can be found in Genesis 37-55.

Often, we look at only the bad that happens in our lives and start questioning God on what He promises to you, not understanding that God will take what was meant for evil and will turn it around for your good, and for the perfecting of the body of Christ. Regardless of what you may be going through or how long it seems to take to receive the promise, if God said, God will see it through.

Get yourself in delivery mode and thank God for all that He has done for you. Remember God made a promise to us in the Psalm of David "Psalm 23:1-6, "that no matter what we go through, He will be right there with us and all His promises are "ye and amen." 2 Corinthians 1:20.

¹ The LORD is my shepherd, I lack nothing.

² He makes me lie down in green pastures, he leads me beside quiet waters,

³ he refreshes my soul. He guides me along the right paths for his name's sake.

⁴ Even though I walk through the darkest valley,[a] I will fear no evil, for you are with me; your rod and your staff, They comfort me.

⁵ You prepare a table before me in the presence of my enemies. You anoint my head with oil; my cup overflows.

⁶ Surely your goodness and love will follow me all the days of my life, and I will dwell in the house of the LORD forever. Psalms 23:4-6

My Life Journey...

I remember this one season after the car accident when I was in prayer, I could hear the Holy Spirit say to me, "Do Not Shrink." I kept hearing that. Later, I was faced with many oppositions that kept coming at me in all different directions, where I was ready to throw in the towel, forgetting all that God had done for me. Thinking that the things that God had given me, were all in Michelle's mind. I started a blog and ended up with over 5,0000 followers called "My Saving Taylor." I started this blog to share my story of what happened to me in the car accident in 2009. It was designed to share words of encouragement, hope, and love of God to whoever was reading it. Unfortunately, I received some criticism that I stopped the blog.

While I was caring for my earthly father before losing his battle with cancer, he asked, "why I wasn't doing my blog anymore?" He continued to say, "Boss (that's what he called me) I couldn't wait to read what you wrote, when I would get up in the morning I would go into my office (in his home) and read your blog. "Man, they would bless me and encourage me that God was in control." I walked away with tears in my eyes not knowing that my own dad was reading my blogs and was being blessed by what God was giving me to blog. I was thinking how dare you stop your blog because of the criticism of others, not at all considering who was being blessed by the blog. My heart was broken that I stopped something that was helping my dad during his time of dealing with cancer.

That taught me to stop allowing other voices to be louder than the voice of God. As I have gone through this journey in my life. I become more God conscious than people conscious. I don't mean that I don't care about what people say because I do, I'm just at a place in my life where I can't, and I will not allow what people think or say about me to change what God has given me to do. I must stay in a place with my heavenly Father where His voice is louder than anyone else's His thoughts towards me are good and not evil. Only He has a perfect end for me.

Stop allowing people to place you in a box. Boxes only give you limited space when God tells you to go out and possess the land. Deuteronomy 1:8 Too many times people break your spirit sharing their own opinion of you, while they are sitting on the sidelines doing nothing; you can't afford to allow others' opinion to take residence in your mind, heart, or soul, because when God says yes, that is all that matters. Only God can open doors that no man can open and make a way out of no way. Put your trust and hope in God and leave it there. In my mother's voice.

My Testimony

❧

When I first began my journey in the ministry. I had all these doubts about not having what it takes to do what the Lord called me to do. I was always looking at my inner ability, insecurity, and my flaws, telling God what I did not have. Wasting so much valuable time, one day the Lord said to me "Michelle it's not what you don't have, but what you do have, give it to Me and I will do the rest."

Stop thinking you don't have what it takes to feed God's people, stop telling Him you need this to do that, and look up to Him. That is where your help comes from, He will take what little you have and multiply it to feed thousands. It's not about what you can do but what God will do through you.

When we take the limits off God, we feed thousands. In the book of Matthew chapter,14:15-2, "Jesus fed 5000 men with five loaves of bread and two fish." The bible says that "They all did eat and were filled" when they took up the leftovers that remained, there were 12 baskets full." Amazing!

Words of my dear friend's mother, "I am a SPECIAL, SPECIAL person" who loves the Lord and wants to please my Heavenly Father by doing what I was purposed to do.

Michelle Taylor

Made in the USA
Middletown, DE
24 March 2022

63132798R00046